Independent Women

DEANNA PINNS-LAWSON
STELLA L. WILLIAMS

Peppertree Press
Sarasota, Florida

Copyright © Deanna Pinns-Lawson and Stella L. Williams, 2009

All rights reserved. Published by *the* Peppertree Press, LLC.
the Peppertree Press and associated logos are trademarks of
the Peppertree Press, LLC.

No part of this publication may be reproduced, stored in a retrieval system, transmitted in any form or by any means, electronic, mechanical, photocopying, recording, or otherwise, without prior written permission of the publisher and author/illustrator.
Graphic design by Rebecca Barbier

Cover art by Sharri Hammersley Jackson

For information regarding permission,
call 941-922-2662 or contact us at our website:
www.peppertreepublishing.com or write to:
the Peppertree Press, LLC.
Attention: Publisher
1269 First Street, Suite 7
Sarasota, Florida 34236

ISBN: 978-1-936051-33-5

Library of Congress Number: 2009932367

Printed in the U.S.A.

Printed November 2009

Dedication

We dedicate this book to Independent Women of the world. Stay strong emotionally, mentally, physically and spiritually!

Acknowledgements

I thank Jesus Christ my savior for giving me another chance. Thanks to my co-author Stella Williams for your patience, intelligence and friendship. Thank you to our editor, Laurie Heins, for your expertise. Thanks to Jo Ann Morgano for being in the right place at the right time. Thank you Myron Enyart for all your support and your loving heart. Special thanks to my wonderful and loving son, Kimani H. Davis, who has always supported and encouraged me in everything. You are the light of my life.

Deanna Pinns-Lawson

I would first like to thank God. Thanks Deanna Pinns-Lawson, my co-author, for all of your wisdom, kindness, friendship, encouragement and support during the time it took to get us to this place, Godspeed. Thank you to our editor, Laurie Heins, tough, but one of the best at what you do. Thanks to Jo Ann Morgano for being in the right place at the right time. Thank you Jerry Williams, my brother, for listening, not judging, and believing that we could do it. A special thank you to Maudie Louise Woods, your spiritual and verbal support means more to me than words can say. A warm and sincere thank you to June Williams, someone special, for your encouragement and support. Much Love!

Stella L. Williams

Independent Women

Who are we?
We are the past
We are the present
We are the future

Who are we?

Table of Contents

Independent Women *(Poem)* 9
3 Generations *(Poem)* 11
Introduction 15
Blind Date *(Poem)* 18
CHAPTER 1: The Dating Process:
    What You Should Know...................................20
    We Smiled *(Poem)* 27
    Why Do I Hold On? *(Poem)* 29
CHAPTER 2: Communication....................................30
    Some Things Never Change,
    or Do They? *(Poem)*... 43
CHAPTER 3: Respect...46
    Untitled *(Poem)*...52
CHAPTER 4: Spending Habits....................................54
CHAPTER 5: Intimacy...62
    HIV/AIDS *(Poem)*...68
    Untitled *(Poem)*...69
    Memories *(Poem)* 70
CHAPTER 6: Resources 72
Conclusion 76
About the Authors 80

Independent Women

Who are we?
We are free as a breeze
We are free as the wind
We are free as the leaves falling
from the trees

Who are we?
We are the past
We are the present
We are the future

Who are we?
We are strong in our thoughts
We are strong within our hearts
We are strong in our spirits

Who are we?
We come in all sizes
We come in all races
We carry baggage

Independent Women

Who are we?
We love
We hurt
We cry

Who are we?
We learn to make choices
We learn to love self

We are Independent Women

Deanna

3 Generations

Left alone when her mother passed away
With only an eighth grade education
Left alone to raise fifteen siblings
Left alone living in an abusive marriage
Feeling angry and afraid, depression sets in
Left alone asking God to heal her pain
Thinking he's the one, she marries again
Left alone learning he smoked and drank
Left alone when she learned she couldn't conceive
Left alone to raise two nieces as her own
Left alone to provide for her new family
Left alone when he died of lung cancer
Left alone fighting for her land
Left alone fighting until the end

Sixteen when she conceived
She carried not one but two in her womb
Torn when forced to marry
Confused and angry with life (her life)
Abandoned her children as if she was
a child again

Independent Women

Returns pregnant
Her dream of becoming a nurse ends
She tries marriage again
Thinks she marries for Love
While traveling all over the world
She bears two more lives

Chooses to control instead of learning
to Love herself
Filled with anger and shame for many years
to come
Running away from her life again
She sells her house and marries her
long lost friend

Married her childhood sweetheart at nineteen
Conceived her only child at twenty
Happy to be married with the Love of her life
Refused to be angry like the other women in her life
Always had a goal and plan to educate herself
Placing her child first in her life
Always said, "I Love You," and not wanting
to repeat the same cycle again
Five years of marriage ends

Lost self in work to avoid the pain
Depressed and alone didn't know where to turn
Two years past she learns to Love herself again
Seven years past she marries the man who made
her laugh again
Mother, wife, caregiver, worker, and college graduate
Watching her son graduate from college
opened her eyes for more
Fourteen years past she loses a part of her life
that made her stronger again

Deanna

Introduction

Many people may wonder what we define as an "Independent Woman." Let us attempt to express our definition here in the introduction.

Today, an Independent Woman (single or married) is an individual who can make her own decisions pertaining to her mind, body, and soul. Independence is freedom within one's self that chooses to have only positive decisions for self. We are financially capable of purchasing our own homes, transportation, and necessities.

Women like our mothers and grandmothers really didn't have a choice as to whether they should or should not be strong working Independent Women. For example, they had to take charge in the areas where their men were not strong or capable. Today, it's not a social stigma for women to decide to remain single, live alone, or to be divorced.

Independent Women

Personally, we would love to have a man take charge of the finances, transportation, home, etc., but that's not the reality for many women. For that reason, some of us must take charge of our own finances, future goals, home, transportation and the list could go on.

Independent means not losing one's identity once one becomes involved in a relationship. For example, don't fall into the trap of becoming a "yes" person, which means to agree with all of his suggestions, plans, and/or arrangements. Also, watch yourself if you begin to see a pattern of taking care of <u>his</u> needs and neglecting your own. We're sure that before you realize what you're doing, a friend or family member will bring this behavior to your attention.

We're not saying that there won't be any give and take in the relationship, because there will, but it shouldn't be so severe that your family and friends start to make comments like, "Where is the Tonya I knew before Fred came along?" or "Has anyone seen Tonya lately?"

Deanna approached me to co-author a book that would inform readers of what it is that we felt an Independent

Woman wants in a relationship. I thought this was a great idea.

We decided to poll some of our male contacts. We asked the question, "From your own experiences, what are the top five things a woman wants from her partner? Please put them in order of priority." Listed below is a sample of the responses we received:

Dean: *Respect, Money, Friendship, Love, Honesty*

Michael: *Love, Vision, Money, Friendship, Christian*

Chestnut: *Job, Understanding, Thoughtfulness, Car, Passion*

Jimmey: *Friendship, Love, Money, Sex, Security*

Chocolate: *Companionship, Support (Emotional), Quality Time Together, Passion/Affection/Consideration, Someone who will listen to her opinions and respect them, even if they disagree.*

John: *Love, Understanding/Communication, Friendship, Honesty*

Ben: *Love, Money, Friendship, Understanding, Thoughtfulness*

From the replies we received, we decided to write about the Independent Woman in the areas of communication, respect, spending habits and intimacy.

Independent Women

Blind Date

You walked into Friday's for our blind
    date looking as unsure as I felt
As you approached me, I could feel your
    uncertainty of the moment
Will she like me?
Will I like her?
To both our surprise, dinner went well
We shared
We laughed
A good time was had
As we said good night with a kiss, I felt
    that this was the beginning of
    something permanent
If not, at least interesting
And interesting it became

Stella

1
The Dating Process:
What You Should Know

The dating process can be a healthy or emotional experience. As in any relationship (dating, engaged, living together or married), one must determine if a relationship is an asset or a liability. A woman wants a man who truly knows himself and is willing to share himself with another individual. Any man able to deliver this will have no problem understanding what his Independent Woman wants from him in their relationship.

Most women want to date one man, but then again, there are those that want to date more than one man. This issue should be discussed at the beginning of the relationship to establish an understanding of what is expected from both parties.

A woman, no matter how independent, still enjoys having her date open and close the car door for her. On a first dinner date, some women might feel it's "the right thing to do" and offer to go "Dutch." However, there are some women who wouldn't even think twice about paying on the first date, or any other date. This is a situation when some of us may think that the man is cheap. Wrong! This is the first date, not a commitment. For those women who are uncomfortable with this situation, express your feelings by letting him know right away.

Communication is one of the most important key factors in ALL relationships. Women want men to listen, not just hear the words. Communicating with one another allows both parties to express how they feel about certain topics, such as respect, finances, children, family and friends. This is the level of communication where you can get a feel or idea of what this person is somewhat like. Do you agree or disagree? Would you like to move on to the next level of the dating process? Sometimes just talking about these issues isn't good enough; women need more. We must really spend some quality time together to see if his talk is bigger than his bite! Listen to "Come Go With Me" by Teddy Pendergrass or "I Wanna Know Your Name" by The Intruders to get an idea of his talk.

Before the "official" commitment, four areas are very valuable to any lasting relationship. The Independent Woman should try to find out as much as she can about the man's style in these four areas during the "dating process."

The Dating Process

1. Communication:
- Does he listen to your opinions and respect them, even if he does not agree?
- Do you feel that he will be able to give you the emotional support you need?
- Does he always have to be right?
- Does he always have to have the last word?

2. Respect:
- How does he treat you in public, at your place and at his place?
- Is he trying to hide you, and even if he's not, do you feel like he is?
- How does he treat you around *your* child(ren), family and friends?
- How does he treat you around *his* child(ren), family and friends?

3. Spending Habits:
Find out his spending habits (as best you can) or even if he can afford to be in a relationship. If not, find out why. Some men are on a tight budget for very good reasons, and while they are moving towards their goal(s), they want someone who is understanding and loving to be in their corner.

If you can handle this type of situation, go for it; but if you can't, be honest and up front about what you need. No need in wasting his or your time, emotions or finances if you can't.

4. Intimacy:

Some people may feel very uncomfortable discussing any intimate details during the dating process, but ask yourself, "When would be the best time to find out if a potential partner is intimate or not?" If you consider intimacy to be an important part of your relationship — in other words, intimacy is something you must have — we would strongly suggest that you think about addressing this issue before you make a commitment.

Other areas to consider:

So, you've decided that he's a good communicator, that he respects you (your child(ren)), that you can accept his spending habits, and that his words (maybe some of his actions) indicate he can be intimate with you. Now you want to move on to the next step, the actual commitment. Before you do, look over the list below:

Make sure you've discussed the topic of HIV/AIDS.

The Dating Process

It's very important to discuss this topic before any physical activity.

- How is his hygiene?
  (teeth, hair, nails and body odor)?

- Can he be easily reached?
  (we realize that some jobs may prevent this)
  or does he disappear for periods at a time?

- Is he needy or controlling?

- Is he jealous of your children, family and friends?

- Is it OK for him to hang out with the boys, but he has a problem when you hang out with the girls?

Concerning his hygiene, we are aware that you may be fooled during the dating period, especially since you may not see each other on a daily basis, but once you have the opportunity to see his living space, check it out carefully! Of course, if he does not want you to see his living space, this is a RED flag that something is not right.

If you answered "Yes" to the last three bullets, boyfriend has a control problem and/or may be abusive. Many Independent Women usually can't stay in this type of relationship for the long haul. We suggest that you may want to think about getting out NOW and

Independent Women

save yourself from being on that "Emotional Roller Coaster" Vivian Green sings about. So, if you have any negative or unsure feelings about any of these concerns, address them before you move the relationship to the next level. If you make the decision not to, he most likely won't change and will think that his actions are acceptable.

The Dating Process

We Smiled

I saw you standing there against the wall
I glanced at you and looked away
But once was not enough,
> so I looked again, this time,
I saw you looking at me
> We smiled

I looked away
A few minutes went by before I got up the
nerve to take another look, only to find you,
Not standing against the wall,
> but at my table right in front of my face
> We smiled

I looked away
Again I waited a few minutes before taking
another look
I located you
Not at the wall, not in front of me,
> but I felt you at my side
I looked up to my right to find you standing
next to my chair asking me if I wanted to dance

Independent Women

A slow dance
The last dance

I took your hand, we slow danced,
and when you Rose, I looked into your eyes
      We smiled

Stella

The Dating Process

Why Do I Hold On?

Why do I hold onto hope when I know
    he's not going to act right?
Why do I hold onto hope when I know
    he's not going to say what I need to hear?
Why do I hold onto hope when I know
    he's not going to give me what I need,
    desire, crave?
Why do I hold onto hope when I know
    he's not going to give me the same
    support I give him?

Why?
Because when I make the decision to pull away,
    he knows.
He pulls me back with a smile, a kiss,
    kind words, or with a sensitive gesture.
Why do I hold on?

Stella

2
Communication

The correct combination of verbal and non-verbal communication is key to any lasting relationship…

When we say the word "Communication," exactly what are we talking about? In relation to the context of this book, we are referring to the communication between a woman and a man in a personal/intimate relationship.

The definition of Communication we would like to share is: sharing information between two independent adults who are willing to listen and not just hear words. Sometimes in relationships there are some misunderstandings, because of the interpretation of the message by the listener who chose not to ask questions. Those questions could be key factors of the relationship. For example, what do you enjoy doing for fun? How do you feel about children? Do you have a relationship with your parents?

Exactly what does this mean to us? First, we must all realize that we will never completely understand anyone ALL of the time, regardless of how long we've known them. There will be situations when trying to communicate will not be an option. During one of these moments, you may have to determine if it's worth the effort to continue to even fight this battle OR just let it pass.

Independent Women

Second, we must realize that some of us can express our concerns and feelings openly and clearly. Others cannot. Some people feel that you should know that a certain word, act, or situation will upset them or make them mad. How? None of us are mind readers. If you do not express your feelings, the other person will have no way of knowing how this situation affected you.

For example, you've just started to talk to this very good-looking young man. In the beginning, the conversations are very smooth and intelligent. You like many of the same things and dislike many of the same things. As time goes on, you start to notice that when he gets angry or is upset with someone, he curses a bit too much for your liking. You make a decision not to say much; especially since he's not cursing at you, but just venting and sharing. The cursing, per say, may not bother you, but when he says, the m... f... words, this crosses the line for you. Now, if you never communicate your feelings, how is he to know that this is a problem for you? You must, from the start, let him know that you can tolerate the other curse words, but this is one word you just can't accept.

Communication

Another example, you've been dating Sean for about two months now and feel that this would be a good time to invite him to your place for a home cooked meal. The date is planned for Friday night at 7:00 p.m.

Friday has arrived. It's about 6:00 p.m. and you're setting the table with flowers, candles, your best linen napkins and wine glasses. You have Marvin Gaye's "Let's Get It On" playing in the background. The smells of his favorite dishes cooking in the kitchen fill the room.

7:00 p.m. sharp, your doorbell rings. You open the door to discover that Sean smells good, looks good, and the best part is, he gives you flowers. Right away you smile and he smiles in return.

What made this date great was your date called you the night before to confirm your dinner plans. Therefore, there was an agreement of communication from both partners that dinner was still on for Friday evening at 7:00 p.m.

Another example, Raye met Wallace during the summer while visiting her aunt in Philadelphia. Raye was

Independent Women

a young sister with a nice personality, funny, long hair, and loved shopping for clothes and shoes. She was in her senior year of high school. Raye had not dated much and thought she knew what she wanted in a relationship. Wallace was a nice looking dark skinned brother, with smooth skin and bright eyes. Wallace was also a sharp dresser and had just graduated from high school.

Raye's aunt knew that Wallace was a nice gentleman and approved of him dating Raye. During this summer vacation, Raye realized that Wallace was a gentleman, quiet, and had a great sense of humor. All this was good, but Raye knew that there was something about Wallace that kept bothering her. But, instead of being honest with herself, for years (yes, we said YEARS!) she avoided expressing her true feelings about Wallace and continued with the relationship. What she realized was that honesty was a large factor in her life. (WRONG!) Communication with yourself is just as important as communicating with your partner. Never stay in a relationship to avoid hurting the other individual.

What Raye failed to realize was that, even though she was taught to always be honest with everyone, she had neglected to be honest with herself. She really didn't want to hurt Wallace, but it was her feelings that were eating inside her. Raye finally told Wallace that their relationship had been a lie, because she really could not get that close to a man of his skin color. (She just did not like dark skinned men.)

There are lessons to be learned from this type of experience. Just because he is nice doesn't mean he is the right guy for you and your preferences.

From our own personal experiences, it's always best to be honest and open from the start of the relationship and let your voice be heard and understood! Don't be afraid to express what you want or don't want. Therefore, if the relationship does become serious, there shouldn't be any surprises, because both partners understand each other. If he does the same, you will both find out early if you have something worth working on. Trying to be someone you're not will only backfire in the long run.

We can also communicate without words, or as we like to call it, "non-verbal connection." One example is: Penny and Jason who were good friends.

~ Independent Women

They had not declared themselves to be in a relationship, but had known each other for about a year and had developed a nice comfortable friendship. Penny found herself spending much of her free time with Jason and visa versa. So this year on Valentines Day, which happened to be a Saturday, even though they were not in a romantic relationship, Penny decided to purchase a nice plant for Jason and took it to his home.

Penny knew that Jason was at work, but left the plant with one of his roommates. Penny did not know that while she was at his house delivering her Valentine's Day gift, Jason had arranged to have flowers delivered to her. When she finally returned home, her mother told her that the lovely flowers she saw on the stereo were for her. Talk about being connected! From that point on they were inseparable.

Another example, Silas and Nicole had dated for a year. Nicole always knew when something was bothering Silas. The night before, Silas and Nicole made plans to go out to a movie and dinner. The night of the date, Silas was more than thirty minutes late picking up Nicole. Silas wasn't himself. He always appeared to be happy when he was around Nicole. Nicole asked, "Is everything OK? You're really late; did something happen?"

When Silas didn't reply, Nicole thought back to the evening before and remembered that Silas had mentioned to her that he was going to stop by his sister's house before picking her up. His sister had something for him to do for her. Nicole, knowing that his sister was jealous of their relationship, wondered if Silas and his sister had an argument.

So, Nicole asked Silas, "Did your sister upset you?" Silas then replied, "We will talk about this later." Nicole wanted this evening to be fun and less tense, so she tried to respect Silas' wishes and didn't express her own feelings. (WRONG!)

While riding in the car, Nicole suggested that they go to their favorite spot at the park. She wanted to talk in private and thought that being at the lake might help. Silas ignored Nicole's suggestion and continued to drive until they arrived at the restaurant where he wanted to have dinner and then go see a movie afterwards. During dinner he apologized for being late.

Independent Women

They were quiet on the drive back to Nicole's home. She realized that this issue needed to be resolved. Nicole tried to explain to Silas how honesty means a lot to her, especially in their relationship. She wanted him to understand that he could trust her. She also expressed that if they could not be honest with each other, then maybe this relationship should not continue.

Nicole was not honest with herself. She made the choice to avoid the real issue. If she had been honest with herself by expressing her true feelings about what the real issues were that they were facing, then maybe things could have been resolved that evening (non-verbal connection).

Sometimes relationships continue only to end, because both parties avoided resolving the real issues by not being honest with one another.

This situation probably could have been resolved if Silas had been honest with his partner. However, he chose to shut down completely instead of addressing the real issues. We call this the non-verbal connecting method.

Communication

The correct combination of verbal and non-verbal communication is key to any lasting relationship, but remember physical communication is also important. Many of us need to know that we are loved; and some, more than others, need to have our partner tell us. We need to hear the words "I love you" with meaning and sincerity.

Sometimes it takes something drastic to make people change. For example, Sally was married to Rich for more than three years. They dated for four years before they got married, so we're talking about having known each other for seven years. Not once during this time period did Rich tell Sally that he loved her. Time and time again Sally expressed to Rich that she needed for him to say, "Sally, you know I love you.", but he never did.

You may be saying, "As long as he is taking care of the home and his business, I really don't care if he ever tells me, 'I love you.'" This may be fine with you, but some of us desire actions and words.

Yes, Rich was working and treated Sally with much respect (the sex wasn't bad either!). But after awhile,

Independent Women

Sally needed for him to say the words and mean them. One day she just had enough and told Rich that she was leaving, which she did. They got back together and Rich had no problem with expressing himself to Sally after that. Today, they are still together and that was more than 15 years ago!

It's a shame that Sally and Rich were heading down the road to a divorce. Lack of communication was a key element in this situation. This issue should have been addressed during their dating process. It most likely was not mentioned because Sally felt that it would work itself out. Many couples say, "I love you" to each other before they say, "I do." Did she miss the clues? Did she have on blinders? Did she feel that it was not an important issue?

Many women and men overlook disturbing behaviors just to keep the peace or push them aside. Unfortunately, they label them as unimportant until they can't take it anymore. For example, if one partner is a very jealous person during the dating period, do you think these feelings will disappear once they are married? We don't think so. Usually, these feelings will build up until she or he can't take the jealously any longer and wants out of the marriage. Issues such as this should always be discussed and corrected when you are dating.

What are we looking for in ways of communicating?

- Someone who can be open-minded.
- Someone who can communicate if his feelings are hurt (yes, men get hurt too).
- Honesty regardless of how bad the situation may be.
- Remembering what's important to you.
- Someone who is willing to compromise.
  (If you want sex 7 days a week and he only wants it 2, can you settle for 4 days?)

If you find that you can't agree, there are a few serious questions you should address:

- Is this the person I want to spend more time with?
- Will it always be his way or no way at all?
- How can we have a future if we can't even agree on what movie to see?

Independent Women

First and foremost, be honest with yourself. Try to avoid stereotyping and always make wise choices. You've heard it before and we must say it again, "Honesty is always the best policy!" Learn from your mistakes and move on.

Communication

Some Things Never Change, or Do They?

    Desire!
    Lust!
    Excitement!
    Respect!
    Friendship!
All describe the relationship we had,
    off and on
    for over 15 years!
Some Things Never Change, or Do They?
Then one day you left without warning.
    No words.
    No letters.
    No calls.
Not a day went by that I did not wonder about how you were doing.
    Are you well?
    Are you still in town?
    Are you in a relationship?
Do you still desire me?

Independent Women

Some Things Never Change or Do They?
I saw you today in the parking lot at Wal-Mart.
It's been four years since you disappeared out
of my life
When you saw me, you came my way.
>   I stopped.
>   We hugged.
>   You kissed me.
>   We talked.
I wanted to ask you:
Are you well? (You still look fine!)
Are you in a relationship? (You didn't say)
Do you still desire me? (Your eyes told it all!)
Some Things Never Change or Do They?
You asked me:
Are you well? Yes
Are you in a relationship? No
Do you still desire me? I didn't say
Some Things Never Change, or Do They?

Stella

3
Respect

The term "Respect" can be misleading for some of us. Before continuing to read, take a minute to write down and answer the following:

- In my relationship with my partner, how would I define respect?
- Think of a situation where you felt you were not respected and write it down.
- What could have happened that would have made you feel like you got the respect you deserved?

Take a minute to look over your responses.

In relationships, how do we define Respect? Your reply may depend on where you are in the situation. Are you the receiver or are you the giver? Either way, respect must be earned and given in all relationships. OK, we're sure that some eyebrows might have risen from the word "earned."

For example, you're on your first date. It's a beautiful summer day, so you decide to take a walk in the park. Of course, you're not alone. There are other people (couples) at the park. Other people are enjoying the lake, absorbing the sun, playing tennis, or picnicking.

Independent Women

Your date, Troy, happens to see someone he knows (female). They say hello and hug like old friends. Does Troy introduce you—NO! Does he explain who she is—NO! Worst of all, she continues to stare while you're trying to enjoy Troy's company, although you're a bit annoyed at his actions. Now, the question you must ask yourself is (remember this is your first date), "Has Troy earned any respect from me?" We would have to answer NO!

This example addresses the questions:

- How does he treat me in public?
- Is he trying to hide you, and even if he isn't, did you feel like he was?

You and your date are learning about each other. You are very secure about yourself; however, if this situation bothers you, address the situation in a matter that your date will understand. Enjoy the time you do have together, and move on. We make our own choices. Therefore, ask yourself, "Is this the right person for me? Who's to say this won't happen again?"

Another way one might define respect is by asking the question, "What type of relationship does Troy have

Respect

with his mother (or if she is no longer living, what type of relationship did he have with her)?" This plays a major part in how he might treat you or think about you.

Later in the relationship, if it gets to that point, make a mental note to plan to evaluate how he reacts around members of his family and "select" members of your family. This may open the doors to continue with the relationship or this might make you run the other way. Always remember, no matter how you may feel about a person, we cannot change anyone!

For example, your partner just down right has NO RESPECT for his mother, regardless of the circumstances. You cannot and should not expect to change this individual by loving him! IT WILL NEVER HAPPEN! He has issues. He has baggage. Unless he realizes these issues for himself and wants to make a change by dealing with the problems, you will not see or hear the word "respect" in that relationship.

Once again, you have a choice. You can dismiss yourself from this person or make the choice to remain in the relationship. Now, don't get us wrong. There are exceptions to every rule. There are men who have issues with

Independent Women

their mother, and because of these issues, have made a decision to treat their ladies like queens.

The term "Respect," can be misleading for some of us. For example, you're riding in the car with your date (Troy) and you're having an enjoyable conversation. You come to a stop sign. Another car stops to the left of you (on the driver's side). Troy turns to look at the car and consciously or unconsciously stares at the male passenger until the car drives off. You notice that Troy is annoyed. You see his body language change. Even after the car has driven away, Troy continues to stare and has obviously forgotten about you, let alone the topic of the conversation. You say, "Hello." This brings him back to you. Of course, by this time you're not sure how you feel, but you do want to know why the passenger in that car has him so annoyed. How would you react? Would you consider his actions to be disrespectful? Would you be jealous? Jealousy is a sickness, and we've all been there.

Respect

Therefore, we suggest that you take the time to express your feelings and explain why you feel the way you do. (Refer to Chapter 2, Communication)

Independent Women

Untitled

It was my (40th) birthday
I wasn't sure if he remembered
I didn't know if he could afford anything

As I walked through his door
He blindfolded me and took me by the hand
We climbed his stairs, they seem not to end
I could hear my heart beating faster, faster, and faster

Not having a clue what was going on
I asked, "Baby, please tell me what are you doing?"
I could feel his smile just by his touch
He sat me down into a chair that I was unfamiliar with

Once he removed the scarf from my eyes
It was as if I was dreaming looking at the stars from a far
It was something beautiful that money could never buy
It was love without a price

Deanna

4
Spending Habits

Many people haven't given much thought to their spending habits and thus do not realize that learning to manage their income would be an asset...

*I*n Chapter 1 we suggested that you might want to find out what you could about your date's spending habits before making an official commitment. Take a minute to think about what YOU need and desire in a partner. Your replies may reflect where you are with your own individual spending habits.

- Do you need someone who knows how to save?
- Do you need someone who is an investor?
- Do you need someone who is "tight" with his funds?
- Do you need someone who is "giving" with his funds?
- Do you need someone to show you how to save your funds?

He might be on a tight budget right now, but you can see that he is working towards goals for the future, which are appealing to you; can you handle this for the long haul?

Many people haven't given much thought to their spending habits and thus do not realize that learning to manage their income would be an asset to them-

Independent Women

selves, their family (if they have children), and any future partner. Of course, all of us are on different levels of spending our income. Some people have no clue. Some people just don't care about saving for tomorrow or for a raining day. Some people understand the need to save and invest, but are not at that place at this time. Some people are just starting out, and the rest are in charge and on top of their financial game. Where are you and where do you need your partner to be?

For example, about three weeks ago, one of your friends introduced you to this FINE young man named Andrew. You are attracted to each other and exchange phone numbers. Your first date was something simple, a movie. Now you're going out on your second date and you have planned a movie and dinner afterwards. (Remember communication is ESSENTIAL.)

Andrew pays for the movie, popcorn, and drinks. After the movie, you hope (or better yet, you really have "assumed," which we should never do) that Andrew will take you to a particular restaurant not far from the theatre. The movie is over, and you're in the car. While discussing the movie, you notice that Andrew

Spending Habits

has just driven past the restaurant you were hoping to dine at.

Now some of us might be thinking, "Has he forgotten we were going out to dinner? Well, maybe he wants to surprise me with something else." By now you notice he's getting on the highway leading back to your place. You make the decision not to say anything. Still wondering what's going on.

At some point during the ride, Andrew mentions that he is hungry and would like to purchase chicken from a fast food restaurant. You weren't expecting this and express to him that you're really not in the mood for chicken, but would rather have a sandwich from a restaurant near your place.

Please keep in mind that this is only your second date, and right now you do not know Andrew's spending habits. He could be on a budget, or he could be thrifty with his money.

As we've discussed in Chapter 2, <u>Communication</u>, the most important chapter of this book, several questions should have been addressed before this date.

Independent Women

First, make sure you both understand that this date would consist of a movie and dinner afterwards.

Second, decide who's paying for the movie and/or the dinner. What movie and where? Where to go for dinner? Will you decide that before the movie or after the movie? Remember, you do not have to wait for him to ask the right questions. You could have addressed the issue of dinner before the movie or directly after the movie simply by asking, "What type of restaurant do you feel like eating at tonight?" This would have opened up the window of opportunity for Andrew to let you know if he had to change the dinner plans.

If you've been dating someone for six (6) months or more, you should have some idea what your partner's spending habits are. Below is a list of things to look for:

- Does he pay his bills on time?
- Is he a saver?
- Is he living from paycheck to paycheck?
- Does he often inquire about your income?
- Does he pay his yearly taxes on time (you may not know this answer yet)?

Spending Habits

- How often in the last month did you go Dutch on a date?
- How often in the last month or two have you paid for the entire date?

Once again, we all have choices. Only you can decide if you want to continue with someone who has bad spending habits, or is cheap. If you make the decision to stay in this relationship, please consider discussing with your partner a way to come up with a reasonable agreement of ways to help him manage his money.

Of course, we are aware that there are some of us who only want a relationship for materialistic reasons. Please remember: Money can't buy you happiness!

For example, if your partner is verbally and physically abusing you and only wants to be intimate with you <u>after</u> he has abused you, can his money erase the scars? Would you still want to continue in this type of relationship? We hope not, and if so, please consider counseling.

What if your partner continues to disrespect you in public and his only means of communication is using

Independent Women

curse words and you know that he is dishonest and sleeps around? Can being involved in any of these situations justify a materialistic relationship? We think not today, or any other time.

It's OK to make mistakes, but learn and grow from these mistakes. Don't settle for less of your self-worth. If you don't remember anything else in this book, please remember this: Continue to use the tools that are given to us. We are ALL rich in so many ways.

5
Intimacy

Another important area in any relationship (men, women, or same sex) is INTIMACY. What comes to mind when you hear the word intimacy? Take a minute to write down your thoughts.

Intimacy between partners can consist of many things. Such as:

- Holding hands
- Kissing each other to say hello or goodbye
- Kissing just because
- Buying him flowers just because
- Receiving flowers just because he was thinking about you or just because he cares
- Just saying, "The time we share together makes me feel complete"
- Talking about feelings, emotions, problems, etc.

Remember Chapter 2, <u>Communication</u>, and take a minute and add two or three actions that you would consider to fall under "intimacy."

A few more would be:

- Calling just to say, "Hello." (Calling, even when you can't stay on the line but for a few minutes, can really make a difference in your relationship.)

- Love notes.

- Holding your partner without any kind of sexual activity.

- Being able to discuss your (or his) sexual likes, dislikes, wants, and needs as they change and/or grow.

- Romancing or being romanced "mentally" first and then physically. If you're in a long-term relationship, at some point, it's going to become very important to be mentally romanced by your partner and/or to mentally romance your partner. There will be times that this will be much more valuable to your relationship than sex.

Intimacy

We believe that the most important factor of intimacy for everyone would be having the freedom to make your own decisions.

To give you an example, if you're in a relationship and it's obvious that you are the aggressive one. You may be aggressive to the point where you are intimate and your partner isn't. However, you have no complaints with your partner in the other areas we've discussed (communication, respect, and spending habits). Now, you have to ask yourself, "Are these areas more important or do I think my partner will change in the future?" Please remember, you can't change anyone. Another thing you must keep in mind is that we as human beings NEVER get everything we are looking for in any relationship.

Ask yourself, "How important is it for me to receive actions of intimacy, and how often?" Only you can answer these questions. Once you know the answers, you can then approach your partner.

Set aside the time to find out why he is not intimate with you. We believe there's a reason for everything. If he says he doesn't have a reason, or just shuts down on you, there's something deeper going on. If he shuts down, don't try to find out why. This will most likely push him further away. Can you handle this, or are you willing to accept it? On the other hand, if he shares his concerns and/or fears with you, can you handle it? Does he want to address them with you? If not, can you handle this, or are you willing to accept it?

If you know that you NEED some degree of intimacy in your relationship, and you truly believe that this aspect is more important than the other three areas put together, a decision must be made. Yes, intimacy plays a large part in our emotions. Therefore, if your emotions are telling you, "No, don't do this," but physically and mentally you are being told, "I need to be honest with myself," it sounds like it's time to move on and get out of this relationship before someone gets hurt. Once again this is called communicating with your partner.

Remember, intimacy consists of the emotional, mental, physical, social, and spiritual aspects of our lives. <u>INTIMACY is not sex, but it can be just as powerful!</u>

If getting physical is your next step, please make sure you have discussed HIV/AIDS. You both should have been tested and be able to show proof

Intimacy

of your results. Once this has happened, then you can make the choice to move on to the next step. Always remember to <u>practice safe sex</u>!

Independent Women

HIV/AIDS

Who knew with a smile on her face
Who knew with a child she bore alone
Who knew the life she chose to live
Who knew the pain she carried within
Who knew the tears she hid
Who knew this wasn't the end

Who knew she could laugh again
Who knew she could feel again
Who knew she could swim
Who knew she could hug
Who knew she was sick again!

Deanna

Untitled

On our first date he expressed his
thoughtfulness with a Lilly, not just any Lilly,
but a Tiger Lilly

Walking side by side he gently takes my hand
    I smiled
    I smiled
    I smiled

When he kissed me for the first time,
I felt butterflies as if I were sixteen again

Realizing that was only the past that went away
to fast

As he rubbed my feet, I felt this was God sent
So I prayed
    I prayed
    I prayed

And I knew right then that this wasn't what
God meant!

Deanna

∽ Independent Women

Memories

Today I didn't recognize you until you spoke
    How long has it been?
    Too long, way too long!
    We smiled
    We hugged
    We talked
    You felt good
    You looked good
    You smelled good!
The good memories came back, like a flood, but then so did the bad
Reminding my heart why we separated so long ago
Later that night, as I lay alone in bed, my body could not let go of the good memories
    Your smile, your eyes, your touch!
        I smiled
        And then I cried

Stella

6
Resources

Independent Women are strong, intelligent and loving individuals…

*I*ndependent Women are strong, intelligent and loving individuals, who need and use different tools to teach, listen, share, connect, bond and learn from each other. How and where can we obtain these tools?

- Start or join a support group
- Use resources from the Internet
- Attend women conferences/seminars
- Enroll in Women Studies classes at your local college/university
- Join church groups/your pastor
- Read community magazines
- Use the library
- Start or join a book club
- Speak to a counselor (college or personal)
- Womanspace, Inc.
- Author's Forum (Barnes & Nobel)
- YWCA
- Women's Opportunity Center
- Search our website at www.dplslw.com

Independent Women

By learning who you are as an individual, you may want to begin by advancing your education, joining a support group, starting a business or just helping women in your community. There is no stopping us (women). Live and learn from each other!

Conclusion

Regardless of our cultures, emotions, expressions, spirits and languages, most Independent Women want their voices to be heard in a personal/intimate relationship. In a relationship, we want to share communication, respect and have intimacy. The level of each of these areas will depend on the two individuals.

Some men have classified Independent Women as being controlling, opinionated and bossy. But, from the other side of their mouths, these same men turn around and say that they don't want a mate that is needy, unemployed, has no car, and the list goes on. "What's a lady to do?" We would tell her, "Do your own Thang!"

Should we give up ourselves to make someone else feel at ease? NO!

Should we give up our voice so that someone else could be heard? NO!

Should we give up our goals and visions of financial and/or educational success to make someone else feel in control? NO!

Independent Women

Someone once asked Deanna, "How can one become an Independent Woman?" Our reply today would be, "An Independent Woman knows who she is as an individual. An Independent Woman realizes what she wants in her relationships and in her life.

She knows her strengths and weaknesses. She has a good idea of what she will bring to the relationship and what she wants her mate to bring to the relationship. She knows how to survive by planning, educating herself and working hard for what she wants, regardless of the arena."

To our male readers, if you decide to get involved with an Independent Woman, be prepared to put down your "manhood" and let her "drive." Sit back and enjoy the ride. Believe us; you will experience the greatest and most challenging ride of your life!

To ALL of our readers, we would like for you to know that most, if not all, Independent Women would like to have a man that truly knows himself and is willing to share himself with another individual.

About The Authors

Deanna Pinns-Lawson has professional experience in the Department of Human Services. She has assisted in churches, community development organizations, government agencies and scholarship foundations.

Ms. Pinns-Lawson was educated at Rider University where she completed a Bachelor of Arts Degree in Liberal Arts and Women Studies. She received the Dr. Mildred Rice-Jordan Scholarship award at Rider University. She is a candidate for the MSW (Master's in Social Work) degree at Rutgers University.

She is the former Founder and CEO for the Single Parents Knowledge Scholarship Organization.

Stella L. Williams was born and raised in Trenton, New Jersey. She holds both AA and BA degrees from Rider University located in Lawrenceville, New Jersey.

Ms. Williams was recognized by the Rider University Women's Studies Colloquium Committee first in 1996 for her student paper entitled, "Folk Magic in the Short Stories of Hurston and Walker" and again in 1999 for her student paper entitled, "A Brief Look into the History of Nursing in the United States With a Look at the Journey of a New Jersey Nursing Assistant."

She currently lives in Central New Jersey.